LOVE GIVES LIFE

A Study of 1 Corinthians 13

Evan May

Copyright © 2012

Golden Mouth Press

All rights reserved. Unless otherwise noted, all Scripture quotations are taken from the *English Standard Version* (Crossway). Cover image by Erik Schmaltz (special font by Rebekah May).

ISBN: 1482016222
ISBN-13: 978-1482016222

What (Some) People Are Saying

If you're like me, you have either heard or taught love from 1 Corinthians 13. You may even think that you have heard most, if not all of the insights of 1 Corinthians 13. I did. That is, until I read Evan May's take on the text. Evan brings us into Paul's thoughts in a clear and engaging way, which is somewhat hard to do. Not only that, he brings clarity to the definition of love which has been hijacked and is now defined as "undogmatic" and "untheological." However, love is very dogmatic and very theological. In a world where social media has made us, "fall for the delusion that what makes us significant is mainly what causes us to stand out from everyone else, rather than what helps us to serve everyone else," what we all need now is a little bit of love, properly understood that is. Read this book!

Curtis Allen
Rap artist *Voice*, author of *Education or Imitation: Bible Interpretation for Dummies Like You and Me*

In this short, helpful book, Evan shows us why love is so crucially important, and why we must pursue love above everything else. If we don't have love, we don't have anything. It doesn't matter how gifted or "spiritual" we are. Evan repeatedly points us to the path of love and shows why love is one of the most important dynamics of the Christian life.

Stephen Altrogge
Pastor, songwriter, and author of *The Greener Grass Conspiracy: Finding Contentment On Your Side of the Fence* and *Create: Stop Making Excuses and Start Making Stuff*

Evan May's *Love Gives Life: A Study of 1 Corinthians 13* is a good example of what Paul says in 1 Cor. 14:26, "Let all things be done for building up." It is brief, unpretentious, but says what must be said to bring the message of the "love chapter" to the heart of the reader. May has been personally moved by Paul's words, and he wants to convey to us the same blessing he has found. He has a wonderful gift for simple, conversational writing, with the most natural and appropriate illustrations. He never assaults the reader, but nurtures him gently, so that we find ourselves growing in grace, almost by surprise. No academic trappings here, but May's understanding of the passage is substantial. I hope that many take the opportunity to learn from this book.

Dr. John Frame
Professor of Systematic Theology and Philosophy at Reformed Theological Seminary and author of the *Theology of Lordship* series

The apostle Paul told his dear friend Timothy, with regard to Christian discipleship, "The aim of our charge is love that issues from a pure heart and a good conscience and a sincere faith." That is, love is the necessary consequence of the Gospel he preached. Today, that charge is unfortunately blanched by all manner of social and cultural influences, reduced to the idea that "love" is somehow synonymous with quiet and unconditional acceptance. My dear friend Evan May looks back to Paul as the apostle reminded his students in Corinth about the true meaning of love, and why it actually changes the world. The study notes Evan has produced ought to sting a little as we remember that somehow the love of God is both patient and unrelenting toward wrongdoing, both kind and truthful, both eternal and immediate. I recommend this study without qualification, and hope to see more from Evan in the future.

Frank Turk
Speaker, writer, and blogger at
www.teampyro.blogspot.com

TO MATT

for training me to put truth to work
on the job of loving people

CONTENTS

	Preface	1
1	Love, Misunderstood and Misplaced	3
2	The Absolute Necessity of Love	13
3	The Distinguishing Characteristics of Love	23
4	The Eschatological Permanence of Love	47
5	Seeking the Greatest of These	59

PREFACE

The subtitle for this book is, quite creatively, "A Study of 1 Corinthians 13." But it would be more accurate to say that this is about 1 Corinthians 13 studying *you*. This is a short book about a chapter of the Bible that I found boring for years (the "love" chapter—see what I mean?), until its message gripped me and pinned me under the weight of conviction. I am presenting this to you because I think it would be quite unfair for you to escape it.

Maybe you are wondering, why another book on love or on 1 Corinthians 13? There is much in print about the excellent way. A few things are unique about this work (not absolutely unique by any means, but perhaps different enough for it to get made fun of by its friends): 1) It is closely tied to the text in an engaging way, without too many abstract pontifications about the quality of love. Surprisingly, many books about 1 Corinthians 13 aren't about…1 Corinthians 13. 2) It is rather brief, but it provides a way of accessing this important chapter without the technical trappings that turn some studies into obstacle courses. 3) You are reading it, which hopefully makes it special enough for you.

And further, this book exists because I wanted to write it, and I wanted to write it for you. One way that we love others in the body of Christ is by using spiritual gifts (1 Cor. 14:1), and one way that authors love readers is by, well, *writing*. If at the conclusion of this short book you feel that it was cruel for me to subject you to it, please know that I had the best of intentions.

Obviously, the standard commentaries on 1 Corinthians were consulted; although they are not credited on every page, they have stealthily made their way into the body of this work.

1. LOVE, MISPLACED AND MISUNDERSTOOD

"...the greatest of these is love."
(1 Corinthians 13:13)

If there is one thing that is prized today, it is *love*. "All you need is love," John Lennon tells us. Love is seen as the fundamental virtue, the primary ethic. Many people hold the most important evaluative question to be, "Is this loving?"

At a restaurant last Mother's Day, I was reminded of this when I looked down at my menu. There was a picture of the owner (or at least I assume that's who it was) standing next to his mom. This was written below their portrait:

> My mother is a minister. But she's not like most ministers you know. In fact, she hates the pulpit. Rather than focusing on theology and dogma, her life revolves around one principle: *loving others*. Case in point: A couple months ago she was driving to a yoga class at 6 a.m. On her way to class, she saw a young man walking down the street. It was raining and it was February. He had on pants and a t-shirt. She pulled over, took him to McDonald's for breakfast, drove him to school, and later that week found him a jacket, a bicycle, and got him plugged into the church community. This is one example of how often my mother finds people who need someone to love them, to show them compassion, and she chooses to live their lives with them. The key word here is WITH them. She calls these people, visits them at their home, invites them to our home, loves them, asks them what they need and does her best

to provide for them.[1]

His mom sounds like a wonderful lady, and I'm sure the individual described was well cared for. But did you notice what he does at the beginning? He places love and theology on opposing sides. He presents as enemies what God has made friends, and what God has joined together let no one separate. You see, love is often the misunderstood attribute, much like an emo kid blogging about life's woes. People have certain assumptions about what love is and isn't, and they tend to speak on its behalf before it has a chance to open its mouth. Here, love is *nontheological* and *undogmatic*. It doesn't have firm convictions. Love is not found in the pulpit but on the street.

For others, love is essentially *nonjudgmental* and *noncorrective*. It doesn't tell people how they are to live their lives but simply embraces them for who they are, no matter their desires or actions. To use the buzzword of the day, love is *tolerant*—with tolerance

---

[1] From a Mothers' Day lunch menu, May 13, 2012.

being understood not as permitting the expression of another viewpoint but as crying uncle in agreement. As Douglas Wilson has noted, the tolerance police have two fundamental tenets: 1) we have an absolute commitment to free speech, and 2) shut up!

So the culture tells us to "just love people," and those seeking doctrinal clarity or moral purity are seen as *un*loving.

This perspective obviously lacks Biblical balance. But if there is anything we learn from 1 Corinthians 13, it is that there *is* something distinguishing about love. There is something unique about it. This chapter is a collection of beautiful statements of the character of love. In fact, I don't have to tell you that; you just feel it as you read the text! But Paul is not rhapsodizing love at random. He didn't just write this chapter so that we would have something poetic-sounding to read at weddings and sing about in songs. This text, like all Scripture, should be read in context. If you tug on 1 Corinthians 13, you quickly find that it is tethered to the rest of the epistle and resists being torn from it. This isn't rocket-surgery, but 1

Corinthians 13 comes between 1 Corinthians 12 and 1 Corinthians 14. There is a reason Paul includes this *here*.

Paul has begun a discussion about spiritual gifts in chapter 12. He has written that the body of Christ is composed of many members with different functions, and that every member's role (no matter how big or small it seems) is indispensable. The hand can't get rid of the foot and expect to be productive, and the eye can't make its exit from the body and hope to have any use except for disturbing Halloween pranks. The Spirit has distributed these tasks throughout the church and has equipped every believer with abilities to serve the people of Christ.

And then, in chapter 14, Paul wants to put forward a principle that will determine how the church operates in spiritual gifts, particularly with prophecy and tongues. That principle is that *everything must be done in the gathered church in order to build up others.* This is the idea he repeatedly presents in chapter 14. It is his constant concern:

"...the one who prophesies speaks to people for their <u>upbuilding</u> and encouragement and consolation" (v. 3)

"The one who speaks in a tongue builds up himself, but the one who prophesies <u>builds up the church</u>" (v. 4)

"The one who prophesies is greater than the one who speaks in tongues, unless someone interprets, <u>so that the church may be built up</u>" (v. 5)

"So with yourselves, since you are eager for manifestations of the Spirit, strive to excel in <u>building up the church</u>" (v. 12)

"For you may be giving thanks well enough, but the other person is not being <u>built up</u>" (v. 17)

Paul encapsulates this in verse 26, *"Let all things be done for building up."* That is the governing rule. But there is an assumed premise in this over-arching principle; it is that, as believers, we *want* to build up others and not simply serve our own interests. In other words, the basic premise is that we would *love* them.

Unfortunately, with the Corinthians (and with you

and me), such things cannot be assumed. Love can be misunderstood, but it can just as easily be misplaced or neglected altogether. And that is precisely why chapter 13 of this letter exists. Paul concludes the previous chapter by saying, *"I will show you a still more excellent way" (v. 31)*. It is the *way* of love. Love is not just another quality that can be tagged on to the list of gifts in 1 Corinthians 12. Love is the very path that leads to exercising those gifts in the way that God intends. Love is the *way* that we use our gifting to serve Christ's people, so that our seeking gifts is really just another means of seeking to love our brothers and sisters.

And yet while the Corinthians, according to Paul, were not lacking in any spiritual gift (1 Cor. 1:7), they were dangerously empty when it came to love. They were spiritually proud; they were self-serving; they were disorderly; their gatherings (as Paul says in 11:17) were not for the better but for the worse; they were triumphalistic; they were trying to one-up each other; there were factions and fights—and all along the Corinthians boasted about their spiritual power.

What Paul wants them to see is that this is not just offset in a manner that needs a minor adjustment; this is *totally backwards*. They were heading in the polar opposite direction from the way of love that Christ designed. And so in chapter 13 he charts this way for them.

If you're fond of summary statements, Paul's idea in this chapter could be expressed like this: *we are to pursue love as we seek spiritual gifts because love gives life to gifts and love outlives gifts.* C.S. Lewis has said that art does not have survival value but gives survival value. Paul seems to have a similar perspective for the relationship between love and spiritual gifts—whatever value gifts have they have by virtue of love, which outlasts them. The first section of the text (v. 1-3) underscores that gifts without love are dead and useless. The second paragraph (v. 4-7) describes what exactly we are to have in mind when we talk about "love." The chapter concludes by contrasting love's eternal nature with gifts' provisional quality (v. 8-13). So we will take these in turn:

- The Absolute Necessity of Love *(v. 1-3)*

- The Distinguishing Characteristics of Love *(v. 4-7)*

- The Eschatological Permanence of Love *(v. 8-13)*

But before we proceed we should read the warning label on Paul's prescription of love. God's Word is here to bring us correction and reproof (2 Timothy 3:16), which means that 1 Corinthians 13 is about to *adjust* us in our attitudes and behavior. This is not comfortable; it involves that painful procedure known as *repentance*. Amy Carmichael has described unlove as a cancer that kills slowly but always kills in the end. There are various treatment options for cancer, and none of them are comfortable. But we don't want to give place to something deadly in our hearts. Are you ready to receive God's remedy?

Unlove is lethal, but love gives life.

2. THE ABSOLUTE NECESSITY OF LOVE

"If I speak in the tongues of men and of angels, but have not love, I am a noisy gong or a clanging cymbal. And if I have prophetic powers, and understand all mysteries and all knowledge, and if I have all faith, so as to remove mountains, but have not love, I am nothing. If I give away all I have, and if I deliver up my body to be burned, but have not love, I gain nothing."
(1 Corinthians 13:1-3)

This text raises a question: what does it mean to be "spiritual"? Is possessing a full array of spiritual gifts *spiritual*? Is speaking with eloquence and persuasion *spiritual*? Is having faith that raises the dead, or lifts a mountain from the earth and casts it into the sea, *spiritual*? Is radical self-denial or courageous sacrifice *spiritual*?

Paul's sobering point in these first few verses is that it is possible to do all of these things and it not be motivated by the Holy Spirit. To be spiritual, it is nonnegotiable to have the *fruit* of the Spirit, the first of which is *love* (Galatians 5:22).

Spectacular gifts without love are insignificant

Paul starts with what the Corinthians apparently valued most—the gift of tongues. If you follow Paul's argument in chapter 14, it is clear that the Corinthians had a particular fascination with this gift, although it often led them to misuse it. So when Paul begins, *"If I speak in the tongues of men and of angels,"* you can imagine that his audience would be getting excited. They are ready to hear what Paul has to say! But then he adds an important qualifier, *"...but have not love* [uh-oh...] *I am a noisy gong or a clanging cymbal* [oh.]."

It is obvious that this is not a flattering description. This jarring phrase reminds me of that famous Saturday Night Live sketch with Christopher Walken egging on Will Ferrell to give him more cowbell in the recording studio.[2] "Guess what? I've got a fever, and the only prescription is more cowbell!" What makes that funny? Well, because no one ever asks for more cowbell! And here Paul is telling the Corinthian believers that they might think they are rock stars when it comes to speaking in tongues, but if they do not have love, they are alone onstage, beating a cowbell.

Then Paul picks two gifts that are particular strengths for him, and he exaggerates them a little: *"And if I have prophetic powers, and understand all mysteries and all knowledge"* and, on top of that, *"...if I have all faith, so as to remove mountains, but have not love, I am nothing"* (v. 2). So the gifts of prophecy, knowledge, and faith, no matter how proficient or effective, without love are totally empty. But notice how strongly Paul puts this. He does not merely say, "If I have all of this prophetic power and knowledge but not love, then my prophecy and knowledge are for nothing." No, he says, "If I don't have love, then *I* am nothing." The person himself is nullified, voided,

---

[2] In Memoriam: Gene Frenkle: 1950–2000.

erased from significance in the absence of love. My life is pointless without love. If in all your capabilities and gifting and creativity you are not loving others, then *you* are *nothing*. This is Paul's point, and it is frighteningly unqualified.

It goes without saying—but since I'm writing this book I'll say it anyway—that Paul's statements run entirely against the current of our culture. Social media (a.k.a. Facebook and Twitter) haven't created the idol of individuality, but they have helped to enshrine it and to catechize its disciples. These platforms encourage focusing on what is distinctive about *me*, what *I* am good at, what people should notice about *my* contribution.[3] And even as Christians we can fall for the delusion that what makes us significant is mainly what causes us to stand out from everyone else, rather than what helps us to serve everyone else. But this is contrary to the very design and purpose of the gifting that God has given us. Richard Gaffin provides a helpful corrective:

---

[3] The italicized *me* and *my*, following a sentence about social media, remind me to tell you that you should search for "Brian Regan Me Monster" on YouTube.

> The way to determine our spiritual gifts is not to ask, 'What is my "thing" spiritually, my spiritual specialty, that sets me apart from other believers and gives me a distinguishing niche in the church?' Rather the New Testament on the whole takes a much more functional or situational approach. The question to ask is, 'What in the situation in which God has placed me are the particular opportunities I see for serving other believers in word and deed (cf. 1 Peter 4:10f.)?' 'What are the specific needs confronting me that need to be ministered to?' Posing and effectively responding to this question will go a long way not only toward discovering but also actually using our spiritual gifts.[4]

The difference, in Paul's mind, is between being a something or a nothing.

---

[4] Richard Gaffin, *Perspectives on Pentecost: New Testament Teaching on the Gifts of the Holy Spirit* (P & R Publishing, 1993), 53.

Radical sacrifice without love is inconsequential

Not a spiritual gifts person? Perhaps you're more of the type calling Christians to live counter-culturally, to care for the poor, to embrace lives of sacrifice—to get off the couch, brush the crumbs off their pants, and *do* something. But Paul says that this too, if it does not come from love, is inconsequential. *"If I give away all I have, and if I deliver up my body to be burned, but have not love, I gain nothing" (v. 3)*.

When Paul talks about giving up his body to be burned, he most likely has in mind the story of Shadrach, Meshack, and Abednego from Daniel 3. They refused to bow down and worship the image of King Nebuchadnezzar but faced the fiery furnace instead. In the midst of incredible opposition, they stood firm with amazing faith and bold sacrifice. And yet it is possible to be just as radical as they were while seeking our own glory and being utterly void of love.

Paul also speaks of giving away all he has, and the term he uses probably has to do with caring for the poor and needy (Rom. 12:20). So Paul is talking about charity work. Interestingly, *charity* is an Old English word for *love*; that is how the Authorized Version memorably renders this chapter. But here he says charity, without *charity*, is nothing. It's possible to live your life as a rallying cry to help the needy and the outcast yet at the end of your days look back upon it all and feel empty.

No matter how special the gift or how extreme the sacrifice, Christian effort that is energized by self-fulfillment and self-love and not pursued for the benefit of others and to the honor of Christ is a *façade*. And God sees right through it. "In this divine mathematics, five minus one equals zero."[5]

Love is like oxygen. It makes no difference how strong your body is; if you don't have oxygen, you're dead. Ineffective. Useless. And spectacular gifts and radical sacrifice without love are nothing. What Paul wants the Corinthians to see is that all of these things can be present and yet the Spirit absent. All of these

---

[5] D.A. Carson, *Showing the Spirit: A Theological Exposition of 1 Corinthians 12-14* (Baker Academic, 1996), 60.

things can be at work and the church be totally pagan. D.A. Carson writes,

> In none of these instances does Paul depreciate spiritual gifts, but he refuses to recognize *any* positive assessment of *any* of them unless the gift is discharged in love. Principally, therefore, any particular gift is dispensable, so far as spiritual profit or attestation of the Spirit's presence is concerned; but love is indispensible.[6]

It is love that distinguishes us as Christ's people. *"By this all people will know that you are my disciples, if you have love for one another" (John 13:35).* They we will know we are Christians by our love, because true love is distinctively Christian. There is a certain scent to love, the striking smell of the crucified Nazarene man. Followers of Jesus bear his unmistakable mark, love shaped in the form of the cross. And, to bring things to the deepest rock bottom (or to the highest mountain peak), love is decidedly Trinitarian. Love demonstrates that we serve the Christian God, who is

---

[6] Carson, *Showing the Spirit*, 61.

a loving Trinity. He *is* love (1 John 4:8). *"The Father loves the Son and has given all things into his hand" (John 3:35).* Love is the family trait, and the children of God necessarily inherit this gene. No love, no Christianity—and no Christians.

The Corinthians should not feel secure in the fact that they have spiritual power, as if that by itself were a mark of spiritual maturity. As Jesus said, there will be plenty of people at the end of time informing him that they prophesied in his name, and he will reply that he never knew them (Matthew 7:22-23). What's the point? You can never diagnose your spiritual health on the basis of your perceived spiritual effectiveness.

These first few verses of 1 Corinthians 13 are terribly convicting to me. I feel something in me, itching for spiritual power, itching for eloquence, itching for confident gifting. And yet what is much more difficult for me to discern is the presence of love. How should you fill-in Paul's sentence? What premise do you need to supply? "If I _____, but have not love, I am nothing."

What about you makes you useful in the body of Christ? What about the way that God has made you tempts you to boast? What is your *thing*? Think about it. And then think about this: how do you use that gifting or that talent or that creativity or that effort as an expression of love for other people? How do you enlist it in your attempts to do them genuine good, to edify them in the faith, to encourage them in the truth? God *has* made you a certain way. The Spirit *has* given you something distinct. That is the point of 1 Corinthians 12. But what he has placed in your hand is a tool for building up the church (Eph. 4:12), not for crafting your own stage. We should get to work. We should tend to our tools, keep them in good shape, sharpen their effectiveness. But we should never forget their purpose.

If I have noteworthy gifts and exert substantial effort, and have not love, I gain nothing. But if I have gifts and I welcome effort and in love I seek to bless others for their joy to the glory of Christ, I inherit the earth.

3. THE DISTINGUISHING CHARACTERISTICS OF LOVE

"Love is patient and kind; love does not envy or boast; it is not arrogant or rude. It does not insist on its own way; it is not irritable or resentful; it does not rejoice at wrongdoing, but rejoices with the truth. Love bears all things, believes all things, hopes all things, endures all things."
(1 Corinthians 13:4-7)

We've seen that Paul holds love to be absolutely necessary. Now he wants to clarify what exactly he means by "love." In verses 4-7, Paul provides a character study of love, profiling its likes and dislikes. He has a series of statements, seven positive and eight negative, describing love's distinguishing features.

I think that this would be a convenient opportunity to take aim at a myth that has persisted in churches and pulpits for some time. The word that Paul uses for *love* here is *agapē*. He uses this noun nine times in this chapter. A common idea that you may have come across is that there is something special about *agapē* love, as opposed to love that is described with other Greek terms such as *phileō*. *Agapē* love is said to be unconditional, Christ-like love, as if that is conveyed simply in the use of the word itself. The problem is that the Bible uses the verbal form of this word to describe Amnon's incestuous infatuation with his half-sister Tamar in 2 Samuel 13:1. And when Paul says that Demas has forsaken him because he *loved* this present world (2 Tim. 4:10), apparently he doesn't get the idea of *agapē* love! On the other hand, in the previous chapter we cited John 3:35, which tells us that the Father *loves* the Son (with the verb *agapaō*); John 5:20 says the same thing, but uses *phileō* without any depreciation of significance.[7]

All that's to say, the kind of Christian love to which Paul is calling believers here is not specified primarily by the word he uses but by the ways he

---

[7] See the discussion in D.A. Carson, *Exegetical Fallacies* (Baker Academic, 1996), 31-32.

describes it, and that's where we'll give our attention. Paul's list in these verses seems to purposefully target the Corinthian church and their problems addressed in this letter. It's like he's painting a portrait of love by using the congregation at Corinth as his negative image, contrasting them at every point. Imagine being present for the first time this letter is read to this church, being able to hear the proverbial pin drop as Paul's depiction of love is communicated, with the members of the congregation looking around at one another in sorrow and shame. Of course, we must see that we are seated right next to them, receiving Paul's admonishment and care.

Love is patient

Paul says that love is patient, or that it is *long-suffering*. The picture is not just that love is able to wait for a long time but that love receives wounds without evening the score. Love rolls with the punches, so to speak. Love does not respond to evil in kind (1 Peter 3:9). It is prepared to overlook offenses when necessary. It does not feel the need to right every wrong done against it. "Love lowers the temperature of most conflicts by refusing to engage in retaliation."[8]

It is evident that Paul has the Corinthians particularly in mind here. The picture that chapter 6 of this letter presents is of a church filled with people ready to take fellow believers to court and air their grievances before the on-looking world. And so Paul tells them, *"To have lawsuits at all with one another is already a defeat for you. Why not rather suffer wrong? Why not rather be defrauded?" (1 Cor. 6:7)*. That is what love does. It is capable of suffering wrong. Love *prefers* to be defrauded rather than tear down a brother and bring dishonor upon the gospel.

Are you prepared to receive injustice? Some Christians seem to lack any category for the fact that they might be *wronged* by someone and that would be the end of the story. Unless the offending party is declared guilty and forced to *pay* (whatever that looks like in their mind), they are unable to recover from

---

[8] Alexander Strauch, *If You Bite & Devour One Another* (Lewis & Roth Publishers, 2011), Kindle Edition, loc. 395.

the situation. But as Christians we are in no position to demand payment! If a fellow believer has sinned against us, Christ has already been punished for it; and if an unbeliever wrongs us, we are to leave it to the wrath of God, who will one day make it right (Rom. 12:19). Obviously, the Bible contains guidelines for reconciling with those who have sinned against us (Matt. 5:23-24; 18:15-17), so Paul is not telling us to just sweep things under the rug and pretend like they never happened. Contrary to the notion of "unconditional forgiveness," Jesus instructs us to forgive our brother seven times a day *if he repents* (Luke 17:3-4).[9] While some offenses may be simply overlooked (Proverbs 19:11), others are to be lovingly addressed (Matt. 18:15). But sometimes, even when the Biblical process for responding to conflict is followed, we aren't happy with the results. The question is, are you okay with that happening? Or will you then come up with your own plan? In such circumstances, love is patient.

---

[9] See Ardel Caneday, "Must Christians Always Forgive?" (Center for Cultural Leadership, 2011).

Love is kind

But love does not merely respond with tolerance in the face of offenses; love is *active* to show goodness to the undeserving. Love, Paul says, is *kind*. And it is generous in its kindness. It is postured to give, to bless, to *demonstrate* love toward others. Love is like a playbook in which every move is designed to be gracious to someone; no matter which play you choose, the only options available to you are to do *good* for them. Love does not wait to decide whether there is something in the other individual that draws out love. Love *leans* forward, assumes the best about them, and treats them as if they are worthy of love.

The distinction between civil toleration of adversaries and a posture of active kindness—and the Grand Canyon leap between them—is wonderfully illustrated in Marilyn Robinson's novel *Gilead*. The story is written as a series of letters from a dying pastor, John Ames, to a child born to him in his age. The letters invite the reader to be an audience of Ames' perspective and concerns. Jack Boughton, the prodigal son of Ames' closest friend and fellow minister, has returned home, forcing Ames to reckon with the wounds that he received from Jack. What becomes clear is that Jack is in need of counsel and care from Ames, but Ames seems unable to get past what he assumes, and even fears, about Jack. He is convinced that Jack has come home only to do him harm, only to spite him, only to be *mean:*

> I don't think I do my heart much good by remembering these things. My point is that he was always a mystery, and that's why I worry about him, and that's why I know I can't judge him as I might another man. That is to say, I can't assign a moral valuation to his behavior. He's just mean. Well, I don't know that that is true of him now. But I do see what he might injure.[10]

Ames is certain that he does not struggle with resentment. "He could knock me down the stairs and I would have worked out the theology for forgiving him before I reached the bottom."[11] But he finds

---

[10] John Ames in Marylin Robinson, *Gilead: A Novel* (Picador, 2004), 184-5.
[11] *Gilead,* 190.

himself immobilized by what he perceives in Jack. Love, however, looks past the unlovable, and sees Christ:

> I fell to thinking about the passage in the *Institutes* where it says the image of the Lord in anyone is much more than reason enough to love him, and that the Lord stands waiting to take our enemies' sins upon Himself. So it is a rejection of the reality of grace to hold our enemy at fault. Those things can only be true.[12]

He finally provides a listening ear to Jack, and he discovers someone broken and needy, not unlike himself. Love is ready to be kind, even to the individuals who create discomfort or uneasiness in us. In the words of John Ames, "Love is holy because it is like grace—the worthiness of its object is never really what matters."[13]

A ready example of such love is available in Paul's own kindness to the Corinthian congregation, a church who had questioned his authority (1 Cor. 1:12;

---

[12] *Gilead*, 189.
[13] *Gilead*, 209.

3:4, 4:18-20), dismissed his speech as lacking eloquence (1 Cor. 2:1-5; 2 Cor. 10:1,), and doubted his apostleship (2 Cor. 11). And yet Paul begins this letter by telling them, *"I give thanks to my God always for you because of the grace of God that was given you in Christ Jesus" (1 Cor. 1:4)*, and he concludes with, *"My love be with you all in Christ Jesus" (1 Cor. 16:24)*. Paul loved this church.

Love does not envy or boast

Love does not envy or boast. Envy is what stirs us to be jealous of others' gifting and qualifications and possessions. Paul rebuked them in chapter 3, *"For you are still of the flesh. For while there is jealousy and strife among you, are you not of the flesh and behaving only in a human way?" (1 Cor. 3:3)*. Love, on the other hand, is not merely human. It is not natural but supernatural, the fruit of the Spirit's work. It does not draw from the resources of this sinful world (things like jealousy and strife) but by the Spirit is armed with heavenly qualities (such as contentment and joy). As Paul will soon make clear (v. 8-13), love is an artifact of the New Heaven and the New Earth, a feature of the restored created order. It is a coin stamped with the currency of the New Jerusalem, reminiscent of the inheritance awaiting us. With love, how can we be envious of others, going about as if we were needy orphans? Love reminds us that we are rich in the gospel, heirs of the King. It frees us from constantly checking the bank account of our lives, comparing the balance with what we see in others.

The flipside of envy is boasting. We can covet the gifting of others or we can boast about our own. Apparently, the Corinthians were doing both. *"What do you have that you did not receive? If then you received it, why do you boast as if you did not receive it?" (1 Cor. 4:7)*. As we said, love reminds us that we are rich, but we are rich *in the gospel.* Not because of our ingenious financial planning. Not because we somehow managed to make it to the top. But because God delights in writing the names of paupers into his will. Grace is eager to shower us with blessings, but it wants full credit. If we find that there is something about us that is exceptional—or even remotely interesting—that is Grace's handiwork.

The Corinthian believers were confident in their spiritual specialties, but they were blind to the pride that made them nasty people. They were so sure of their own capabilities that they were convinced they needed neither Paul's wisdom nor his correction. *"Some are arrogant, as though I were not coming to you." (1 Cor. 4:18).* This is not the way of love.

Love is not arrogant or rude

Thus, Paul says in his next statement that love is not arrogant or rude. *Arrogant* translates an idiom for being "puffed up" or being a "windbag." Paul uses a similar expression earlier in the letter: *"Now concerning food offered to idols: we know that 'all of us possess knowledge.' This 'knowledge' puffs up, but love builds up." (1 Cor. 8:1).* This is how Paul introduces the discussion about Christian liberty. The hotly debated question in the Corinthian congregation involved whether it was morally permissible to eat meat that had been sacrificed to idols and then subsequently sold in the market place. Some believers were unconcerned about this practice, but others (perhaps due to a pagan background) had consciences that would not allow them to partake of such meat. The problem, as Paul describes it, was that certain members of the church had accurate knowledge (that an idol has no real existence and that eating food sacrificed to them is not sinful), but they were puffed up with this knowledge and were arrogantly critical of the weaker believers who held to more strident moral standards. They held their own liberty as if it were an inalienable right and failed to demonstrate any love to their brothers and sisters.

This is a common temptation in the church today. We encounter people who have different convictions than we do, who don't approve of something that we think is fine, and we are tempted to dismiss them or judge them because we feel that they look down on us. We think they're foolish or naïve or goody-goodies (or worse—"fundies") because they won't go to the places we go or see the movies we see or listen to the music we like. Well, even if our knowledge is accurate that it is permissible to do these things, so what? What is it good for if it causes us to arrogantly disdain our fellow believers in Christ? Love is not puffed up.

And it is not rude. Listen to how Paul describes this church's gathering for the Lord's Supper: *"When you come together, it is not the Lord's supper that you eat. For in eating, each one goes ahead with his own meal. One goes hungry, another gets drunk. What! Do you not have houses to eat and drink in? Or do you despise the church of God and humiliate those who have nothing? What shall I say to you? Shall I commend you in this? No, I will not." (1 Cor. 11:20-22)*. How rude! Now, it's easy to recognize how pathetic this scenario is at Corinth. What is more difficult to perceive is how this is present among us. Love defers to others. Love does not come to a church gathering with its own agenda, demanding comfort and responding with irritation and rudeness when someone hinders that. Our consumer culture has coached us to approach everything with an eye to how *we* can be served, what can be done for *us*. And it is with this posture that we often come to church. What happens if someone has taken the seat you prefer to sit in, or parked in your favorite parking spot, or poured the end of the coffee pot into their cup? What dictates your attitude in that situation? Is it love?

Love does not insist on its own way

Love does not insist on its own way or, stated differently, it is not self-seeking. People are (rightly) fond of quoting Paul's statement, *"Whether you eat or drink, or whatever you do, do all to the glory of God" (1 Cor. 10:31)*, but this too has a context. This is from the portion of the letter (chapters 8-10) in which Paul addresses, as we've seen, food sacrificed to idols and the issue of Christian liberty. In the heated discussion at Corinth, too many believers were insisting on their own way, being certain of their own understanding, and they were demanding agreement from their fellow church members—whether or not it offended their consciences. "You don't like it when I eat meat sold in the market after it's visited the pagan temple? Well, deal with it!"

What Paul wants them to see is that, even though this is a matter of eating and drinking, this is not morally neutral.[14] Everything must be done to the glory of God. More precisely, God is glorified when we abandon our own liberties for the benefit of our brothers and sisters. Here is Paul's full statement, with his careful nuances and directions:

> *"'All things are lawful,' but not all things are helpful. 'All things are lawful,' but not all things build up. <u>Let no one seek his own good, but the good of his neighbor.</u> Eat whatever is sold in the meat market without raising any question on the ground of conscience. For 'the earth is the Lord's, and the*

---

[14] The traditional label of *adiaphora* ("indifferent things") is not very helpful. It is true that, whatever Scripture does not condemn (either explicitly or implicitly) is not sinful (at least in and of itself), and therefore in that sense it is "indifferent." But the vision of the Christian life that Paul presents in this discussion is that *nothing* is indifferent. *Everything* must be done for God's glory and for the good of others. As Abraham Kuyper has said that there is no square inch in all of creation over which Christ does not declare, "Mine!", the same is true of every aspect of our lives. Nothing is neutral with respect to Christ's lordship. Whether we eat or do not eat, indeed, "whether we live or whether die, we are the Lord's" (Rom. 14:8).

fullness thereof.' If one of the unbelievers invites you to dinner and you are disposed to go, eat whatever is set before you without raising any question on the ground of conscience. But if someone says to you, 'This has been offered in sacrifice,' then do not eat it, for the sake of the one who informed you, and for the sake of conscience— I do not mean your conscience, but his. For why should my liberty be determined by someone else's conscience? If I partake with thankfulness, why am I denounced because of that for which I give thanks? So, whether you eat or drink, or whatever you do, do all to the glory of God. <u>Give no offense</u> to Jews or to Greeks or to the church of God, just as <u>I try to please everyone</u> in everything I do, <u>not seeking my own advantage</u>, but that of many, that they may be saved" (1 Cor. 10:23-33).

In chapter 9 Paul had listed the ways that he had given up his own rights for the profit of those whom he serves. Love does not seek its own advantage but welcomes every sacrifice for the good of others.

Love is not irritable or resentful

Love is not irritable; it is not quarrelsome or easily angered. It is not ready to go at it in a fight at the first signs of insult. In other words, love is the opposite of the conflict-ridden atmosphere at Corinth (1 Cor. 1:10-11).

Love is not resentful, or as some translations render this, love does not keep a record of wrongs. Love prohibits us from keeping a personal file of all the individuals who have done something against us. How do you know if you keep a record of wrongs? Simple. When you see someone, what comes to your mind? Are you immediately confronted with the fact that you just don't like that person because of something they've said or done? Or are you ready to show love?[15]

Ultimately, it is only the gospel that can transform us from people who nurse grievances to those who clear out from our hearts any lack of affection toward others because of how they've hurt us. God does not

---

[15] As the fellow says, "Every man should keep a fair-sized cemetery in which to bury the faults of his friends."

keep a record of wrongs against us; he destroyed that record, nailing it to the cross (Col. 2:14). In fact, *"in Christ God was reconciling the world to himself, not counting their trespasses against them" (2 Cor. 5:19).* In the gospel God lost, if you will, his ability to do arithmetic; he lost count of the grievances that we had done against him because the blood of the Savior covers them all. He holds not one against us. The statement of our debt is stained by Christ's blood and pinned to Calvary's tree for eternity.

Love does not rejoice at wrongdoing but rejoices with the truth

Love does not rejoice in wrongdoing. This could mean celebrating and giving approval to sinful practices (Rom. 1:32), which some in this congregation seemed to be doing: *"It is actually reported that there is sexual immorality among you, and of a kind that is not tolerated even among pagans, for a man has his father's wife. And you are arrogant! Ought you not rather to mourn? Let him who has done this be removed from among you" (1*

Cor. 5:1-2). This is further evidence that the Biblical understanding of love clashes with cultural assumptions, since here love involves kicking someone out of the church! Sometimes, the duty of love necessitates the redemptive discipline of professing Christians who persist in unrepentant sin. Love makes appropriate distinctions between right and wrong, light and darkness, between what honors God and what displeases him. Note that Paul is calling this church to a measure of intolerance; he speaks of practices that are *"not tolerated even among pagans,"* while welcomed at Corinth—with the implication being that they should stop tolerating them!

Rejoicing in evil could also mean being overjoyed at the fall of another, or being vindictive when it comes to the wrongdoings of others. The quintessential representation of this is taking someone to court and having them pronounced *wrong* and celebrating the verdict. We've already seen that this was a common practice for the Corinthian church. But this can happen on a smaller scale. When you discover that someone you don't particularly enjoy has fallen into sin or struggles with a certain weakness, does it make you happy?

Sometimes it makes me happy. Which is why I'm desperate for God to work this text into me!

Love is omni-enduring

Love is omni-enduring. That is my summary description for Paul's statements in verse 7. There is a certain cadence to the text: Love *always* bears, it *always* believes, it *always* hopes, it *always* remains.[16] It is omni-enduring, despite whatever it faces. Stated another way, love is designed to put up with everything, not in a way that minimizes sin or ignores falsehood (which would not be Biblical love), but in the sense of withstanding the opposition of others with grace-filled persistence for their good. Love is not overcome by resistance. It remains ready to show love to the undeserving, even in situations that appear

---

[16] Rendering what is often translated as "all things" (*panta*) adverbially. Cf. Smart guys.

hopeless. Robertson and Plummer write, "When the evidence is adverse, love hopes for the best. And when hopes are repeatedly disappointed, it still courageously waits."[17]

Providence had it that as I typed this section, a friend stopped by my desk, not hiding his tears. He stood there awkwardly, without speaking, but it was clear what had taken his thoughts. His wife of twenty-three years had been contemplating the idea of leaving him for another man. When he finally spoke, he said, "It's so hard to have hope." So I read him verse 7. Love always hopes. It courageously waits.

Love is active

Now, something interesting to note is that in all of these descriptions of love in verses 4-7, at each point a *verb* is used. In several cases this is rendered in English with an adjective (it doesn't work to say that love *"patiences"* or *"kinds,"* so we say that love *is*

---

[17] Archibald Robertson and Alfred Plummer, *A Critical and Exegetical Commentary on the First Epistle of St. Paul to the Corinthians* (ICC: T. & T. Clark, 1911), 295.

patient or kind). But what we have in the original text are fifteen verbs stating what love *does*. Love is active. It is on the move, in forward motion. And what we should see is that in none of these descriptions is the *feeling* of love primary. I don't know about you, but this is freeing for me. 1 Corinthians 13 is not calling us to wait until we feel like loving people before we demonstrate love to them. It's telling us to *love* them.

With reference to marriage, Timothy Keller writes this:

> Our culture says that feelings of love are the basis for actions of love. And of course that can be true. But it is truer to say that actions of love can lead consistently to feelings of love. Love between two people must not, in the end, be identified simply with emotion or merely with dutiful action. Married love is a symbiotic, complex mixture of both. Having said this, it is important to observe that of the two—emotion and action—it is the latter that we have the most control over. It is the action of love that we

can promise to maintain every day.[18]

We may not have ready control over our emotions. But we can control what we *do*. Love is not mainly about having a fuzzy feeling for people. Paul is saying that if your motive is love, get out and *do* love for them. Paul is prescribing action for us in this text. And it is very clear how to apply it.

The final description in verse 7 about love always enduring sets up the next major paragraph about the permanence of love.

---

[18] Timothy & Kathy Keller, *The Meaning of Marriage: Facing the Complexities of Commitment with the Wisdom of God* (Dutton, 2011), 95.

EVAN MAY

4. THE ESCHATOLOGICAL PERMANENCE OF LOVE

"Love never ends. As for prophecies, they will pass away; as for tongues, they will cease; as for knowledge, it will pass away. For we know in part and we prophesy in part, but when the perfect comes, the partial will pass away. When I was a child, I spoke like a child, I thought like a child, I reasoned like a child. When I became a man, I gave up childish ways. For now we see in a mirror dimly, but then face to face. Now I know in part; then I shall know fully, even as I have been fully known. So now faith, hope, and love abide, these three; but the greatest of these is love."
(1 Corinthians 13:8-13)

If at the moment you're thinking, "Escha-wha…?", we'll get to that soon.

We could summarize these verses (v. 8-13) with this proposition: *love is superior to gifting because gifting is temporary but love is eternal.* Paul takes these two items, love and gifts, and he places them on the scale of eternity and steps back to let the Corinthians see the results. Note the contrast in verse 8: *"Love never ends. But as for prophecies, they will pass away; as for tongues, they will cease…"*

Now, Paul is making some beautiful and powerful statements here, but sometimes they are missed because we get caught up in a debate over these verses and whether they teach a theological position called *Cessationism*. So, we'll address that briefly and then move on to the main point. Cessationism is the belief that certain spiritual gifts such as prophecy and tongues *ceased* after the time of the apostles and the closing of the New Testament canon. Cessationists would understand the nature and purpose of these gifts differently than Continuationists (those who believe that these gifts *continue* to be distributed), and from their perspective it would undermine the sufficiency of Scripture if they were practiced today. Some Cessationists cite this text in support of their belief that these gifts have ceased, since Paul talks about prophecy passing away and tongues ceasing and the partial giving way when the perfect comes. On this understanding, the perfect is a reference to the completed Bible. Once the process of inscripturation is finished, certain gifts are no longer necessary.

The problem with this reading of the text is that it is fairly clear what Paul has in mind here. Paul is contrasting the state of affairs in this present world with the way things will be at the return of Christ and the experience in the New Heaven and the New Earth. The contrast is between *now* and *then*, between the limited knowledge and perspective achieved in this age and the understanding that will be enjoyed in the age to come. To see the "perfect" as referring to the completed Biblical canon reads a concept into the text that isn't present in this context, and it causes Paul's statements about "seeing face to face" and "knowing fully" to become rather hyperbolic.

Cessationist author Samuel Waldron agrees and writes:

> Not a few Cessationists have attempted to

defeat this argument by denying that the perfect is the condition ushered in by the Second Coming of Christ. They argue instead that the perfect is the condition ushered in by the completion of the canon. Though I esteem those of my fellow Cessationists who hold this view, I cannot accept their arguments. It seems clear to me that verse ten and verse twelve are parallel: 'For now we see in a mirror dimly, but then face to face; now I know in part, but then I will know fully just as I also have been fully known.' To me, verse twelve seems clearly to refer to the condition of the eternal state ushered in by Christ's Second Coming (2 Cor. 5:7; 1 John 3:2). On this point of interpretation I agree with the Continuationists.[19]

So, whether or not a case for Cessationsim can be made on other grounds,[20] this text is not the best

---

[19] Samuel Waldron, *To Be Continued?: Are the Miraculous Gifts for Today?* (Calvary Press, 2007), 63.

[20] For the traditional arguments on all sides, see *Are Miraculous Gifts for Today?: Four Views*, ed. Wayne Grudem (Zondervan, 1996).

choice.

However, that is not to say that 1 Corinthians 13 doesn't refer to the cessation of spiritual gifts. On the contrary, Paul's point is that spiritual gifts *have* an expiration date. They *will* cease. But they will ultimately cease when the world is made new, when what is partial yields to what is perfect.

The Bible presents history as heading toward a goal. There is a grand conclusion to it all. Unlike the Hindu and Buddhist worldviews, Biblical history is not cyclical. It is linear. And it is ramping up toward something. The fancy word for this is *eschatology*, the doctrine of last things. There is an end in sight, and it is called the *eschaton* (1 Peter 1:5). Jesus Christ will break through the clouds with a loud shout and will summon his people to himself, and together we will enter a glorified state and a creation lifted from the curse in perfect communion with the Lord forever. That is the blessed hope (Titus 2:13), what every believer is anticipating. This is what Christians get excited about! That is not yet, but it will be.

And what Paul is saying here is that on that day, love will enter the renewed world, but spiritual gifts will be left behind at the door. To put it technically, gifts are *subeschatological,* while love is eschatologically enduring.[21] It remains forever.

Look at what he says: *"Love never ends. As for prophecies, they will pass away; as for tongues, they will cease; as for knowledge, it will pass away. For we know in part and we prophesy in part, but when the perfect comes, the partial will pass away" (v. 8-10).* Paul is contrasting what is "in part" with what is perfect or complete. Things that belong to the realm of the partial have not yet reached their goal. They are *im*perfect, *in*complete. This world has not yet matured to perfection, and that will not happen until our perfect Christ returns (1 John 3:2).

But the key thing is that Paul locates gifts of prophecy, tongues, and knowledge—along with all spiritual gifts—in the category of the *partial.* This is

---

[21] Richard Gaffin, *Perspectives on Pentecost,* 44. Gaffin helpfully distinguishes between the *gift* of the Spirit, which is an eschatological reality brought from the future into the present (Acts 2:17; Rom. 8:23; 2 Cor. 1:22), and the *gifts* of the Spirit, which are subeschatological and provisional.

how he articulates the contrast: *"When I was a child, I spoke like a child, I thought like a child, I reasoned like a child. When I became a man, I gave up childish ways. For now we see in a mirror dimly, but then face to face. Now I know in part; then I shall know fully, even as I have been fully known. So now faith, hope, and love abide, these three; but the greatest of these is love" (v. 11-13)*. Here is the irony: while the Corinthians thought that they were "advanced" spiritually because of their success with spiritual gifts, Paul says that they lack what is truly advanced, *love*. Rather, what they possess, *gifts*, are not of the character of eschatological maturity but of being a child. That is the current state of things.

Now, that isn't a negative picture; Paul isn't calling spiritual gifts "childish" in the way that we normally use that term. In fact, he includes himself, with all the revelation he's received, among those knowing limitedly—like a child standing on his toes trying to see above the counter.[22] But the point is that certain

---

[22] Note the first person plural pronouns in verses 9 and 12: "...*we know in part and we prophesy in part...we see in a mirror dimly.*" Even inscripturated revelation is among the partial knowledge experienced in this life!

activities accompany certain ages. *Now*, we peer into the future world through an aged window, and we have spiritual gifts. *Then*, we will gaze into his glorified face, and we will still have love. He is drastically reorienting their values. They did not posses love, and they seemed to be disturbingly unconcerned about it.

The Corinthians held to what is sometimes called an "over-realized eschatology." They thought that their spirituality meant that they had already entered the age to come, and the effect of this idea is noticeable throughout this letter. They thought that their church was an expression of heaven on earth because of their power and their eloquence and their class. But Paul's argument in this chapter is that gifts are not for the age to come, not for the future *eschaton*, but for now. Love, however, is both for *now* and for *then*, and yet love was the very thing they were missing.

This is not at all to imply that gifts are unimportant. The fact is, we still live in the present (to state the obvious). So we still need spiritual gifts. Cessationists and Continuationists agree on this point.

Pursue love *and* earnestly desire spiritual gifts, Paul writes at the beginning of the next chapter (1 Cor. 14:1). Gifts are *very* important. But they are of *relative* unimportance when compared to what is *ultimately* important.

In the New Heaven and the New Earth, we will not need teachers, because we will know fully even as we are fully known. We will not need healing, because we will live in bodies that are unable to experience illness. We will not need hospitality, because we will always be at home. We will not need gifts of mercy, because all of our needs will be provided for. And we will not need the gift of faith, because we will see him as he is. This is what Paul anticipates: face to face, with the risen Christ, embracing him only with love. Everything partial will be removed until the influence of the perfect reaches every surface of the renovated cosmos, and love will shine with warmth on every hill of the New Jerusalem.

Paul wants the Corinthians to view every aspect of their life and calling, even spiritual gifts, in light of this eternal perspective.

There is a particular couple that regularly reminds me of love's eschatological permanence. John Piper's ministry *Desiring God* recently featured a video about the story of my wife Rebekah's cousin Ian and his wife Larissa.[23] Ian was in a car accident several years ago that left him with significant brain damage and the loss of several functions, including the ability to walk and to speak clearly. Throughout the time of Ian's experience in the hospital and his slow recovery, his girlfriend Larissa was always by his side, and they were eventually married.

In the video, Larissa speaks about how significant Piper's book *This Momentary Marriage* is for their relationship.[24] You see, marriage is also called a *charisma* in 1 Corinthians 7, a gift that will pass away. It is partial. My marriage to Rebekah, and Larissa's marriage to Ian, will not be a feature of eternity. And in the present, Larissa is faced with the challenge of living in a marriage that is marked by discomfort and

---

[23] This video can be viewed at http://www.desiringgod.org/blog/posts/the-story-of-ian-larissa.
[24] John Piper, *This Momentary Marriage: A Parable of Permanence* (Crossway, 2009).

suffering, and above all the absence of "normalcy." And yet she welcomes this with joy, knowing that it won't always be this way.

The tagline for Ian and Larissa's blog (www.prayforian.com) is from 1 Corinthians 13: *"Now I know in part; then I shall know fully."* In the New Heaven and the New Earth, Ian's disability will not remain. He will not be entering the new creation with a wheel chair or with brain damage. In the *eschaton*, Ian and Larissa's marriage will be returned to Christ, and their relationship will no longer be defined in that way. Their marriage will have been *momentary*, permanent with respect to this life and temporary with respect to the next. At Christ's return, the strong faith that Ian and Larissa have clung to will be released like a bird to ride the skies of the New Earth on the wings of sight.

But what will remain is love. The sacrificial love that Larissa has shown Ian will have the privilege of entering the restored created order. It will be a special guest at the wedding feast of the Lamb.

Love gives life to gifts, and love *outlives* gifts.

5. SEEKING THE GREATEST OF THESE

"So now faith, hope, and love abide, these three; but the greatest of these is love. Pursue love…"
(1 Corinthians 13:13-14:1)

The smoky scent alerted Christy's attention, which had wandered out the door and was making its way for the street. She flipped the pancake, black side up. Since Christy is always searching for metaphors, she thought that the burnt breakfast appropriately characterized her relationship with Joe, who was snoring in bed and probably drooling on the pillow. Like the pancake (she thought, converting her metaphor into a simile), their marriage was so promising, but it had quickly become a merry-go-round. She was mixing metaphors now, like she had mixed the pancake batter, so she abandoned the exercise and gave full contemplation to how unhappy she was feeling. Every day was chore after chore. And then there were the kids. And Joe didn't seem to understand or really care. The only time he looked vaguely interested about life was when he talked about work. And then the thought came, something she would never speak but was clearly thinking—"I don't love him anymore."

"These two are so pathetic!" John said out loud as he raced through another yellow light, running late for the conciliatory meeting. John and a couple of other deacons agreed to meet with two members of the church who had hit an impasse in their attempt to settle a financial dispute. The first meeting seemed to go really well; both parties were ready to submit to a process of determining the details of the situation. But after that they dug their feet in, each maintaining that they were in the right and giving no signs of movement toward one another. It wasn't long before "prayer requests" were being spread among the congregation, expressing concern for the fellow believer who was doggy-paddling in sin. The last appointment had been about as comfortable as taking a bath with a middle-aged cat. "Such are the trials and tribulations the righteous must face," John joked to himself cynically as he pulled into the parking spot at the church building.

The phone rang, and as Sandy turned over to answer it, she noticed that her alarm clock registered two in the morning. Eric's probation officer was on the other end, informing her that her son had been picked up on another drug charge. She thanked him for calling, hung up the phone, and switched off the light, pretending that she could fall back asleep. She had had enough, and understandably so.

While these three stories convey unique challenges for the fictional individuals involved, each one is about the need to love difficult people. As we have seen, Paul's "hymn of love" is not intended to be lifted from its earthy context in order to float a few feet above ground as something we look up to and admire. No, this text is staked into the soil of a dirty congregation, and it is aware of the fallen-world realities that touch it. Love does not come without challenge, from both the obstacles of others and the objections in our own hearts. Paul knows this, the Bible knows this, and God knows this. And I bet you know it.

At the same time, we cannot be rescued from the fact that the standards of the excellent way are high. This is, in many respects, a list of impossible qualities. But Paul permits no excuses.

There is hope, however! If this did not come with hope, this would not be a Christian book. In Christ we have the perfect portrait of the love of God (Col. 1:15; Heb. 1:3), and in the Spirit we have a flawless artist who crafts us into that image (Rom. 8:29; 2 Cor. 3:18).

Love became flesh and dwelt among us, and we have seen his glory, the glory of the only Son from the Father, full of grace and truth. God so loved the world that he sent Love into the world. Love clothed himself in human form and wrapped a towel around his waist to stoop and wash muddy feet. He did not come to be served but to serve, and to give his life as a ransom for many. He entered a cursed world to love the utterly unlovable, setting his affection and care on the diseased, broken, and self-destructive. He took upon himself our unbelievable selfishness and bore the weight of our empty love, burying it with him in the grave. And Love has risen with healing in his wings.

That Love gives life. Love incarnate has become a life-giving Spirit (1 Cor. 15:45), generating in us the order of renewal. There is a new pattern, a new template, for love—and we are crafted according that portrait by the Spirit. *"And we all, with unveiled face, beholding the glory of the Lord, are being transformed into the same image from one degree of glory to another. For this comes from the Lord who is the Spirit" (2 Cor. 3:18).* We behold the glory of the Lord Jesus and are transformed into that glory by the Lord Jesus, who is the Spirit. This is not Trinitarian confusion on Paul's part. The works of the Second and Third Persons of the Trinity are in such harmony that they are nearly identical. They are after *you*, redeemed and changed. The Spirit is Jesus' *acting presence* among us, producing in us his desires and likeness.

The positioning of 1 Corinthians 13 in the context "concerning spiritual things" (1 Cor. 12:1) is not accidental. The fruit of the Spirit is love (Gal. 5:22). Love is unavoidably Spiritual, with a capital "S." It is a distinguishing indicator of the Spirit's presence in a church. No one says, "Jesus is Lord" except in the Holy Spirit (1 Cor. 12:3), and no one submits to his lordship in the calling of love (with all the sweeping demands we've witnessed) apart from the Spirit's doing.

Now, in case these statements are messing with your equilibrium and about to give you a nosebleed, let it be known that these are not esoteric concepts but foundational realities for change. If you want to be more loving, it won't happen apart from this. But it *can* happen because of this. The work of Christ, applied by the Spirit, means that we can become radically loving people. Paul tells us to pursue love, and this is something that we are able do. He makes clear at the beginning of this letter that he is writing to *"those sanctified in Christ Jesus, called to be saints together with all those who in every place call upon the name of our Lord Jesus Christ, both their Lord and ours" (1 Cor. 1:2)*. The Spirit sanctifies us in Christ and calls us under his lordship. That does not make change *easy*, but it does make it *available*.

What relationship is in desperate need of attention from what you have learned from this text? Is it your marriage? Is it a friendship? A relative? A member in your congregation? What individual are you reluctant to love, tentative with your kindness, distributing it in small pieces so that you don't risk disappointment? Is there someone that you are often tempted to dismiss? Someone that causes you to speed-up your walk when you see them in the hallway? Who is it that makes you jealous or angry when you think of them?

Whom has Christ called you to love?

The thirteenth chapter of 1 Corinthians is about having a *love strategy*. Paul relativizes what we tend to value most (usually our personal distinctives and niches), places love in central view, and summons us to use every power and resource we have for the good of those whom God has placed in our lives. This is the excellent way of love, and it is worthy of our pursuit. It comes with great cost, but it is a treasure hidden in a field.

> Love can hurt like a blast from a hand grenade
> When all that used to matter is blown away
> There in the middle of the mess it made
> You'll find a good thing[25]

Dig through the mess. Love, and find life.

---

[25] Andrew Peterson, "Love is a Good Thing," *Resurrection Letters: Volume II* (Centricity Music, 2008).

ABOUT THE AUTHOR

"I have been crucified with Christ. It is no longer I who live, but Christ who lives in me. And the life I now live in the flesh I live by faith in the Son of God, who loved me and gave himself for me."
(Galatians 2:20)

Evan May is a student at Reformed Theological Seminary and a pastor at Lakeview Christian Center in New Orleans. He is married to his best friend and fellow bibliophile Rebekah and has one daughter, Piper.

www.evanemay.com

Twitter account: @evan_may.

NOTES

NOTES

NOTES

NOTES

NOTES

Printed in Great Britain
by Amazon